More Than

ABANDON YOUR LABELS, EMBRACE YOUR CALLING

VONAE DEYSHAWN

VONAE DEYSHAWN

ISBN: 0692265074
ISBN-13: 978-0692265079 (Virtue Media)

DEDICATION

This book is dedicated to every woman who has ever felt less than worthy. To my parents, siblings, husband and precious baby boy. Thank you for believing in me even when it was hard to believe in myself.

CONTENTS

1   It All Starts With Identity   1

2   Make No Mistake   12

3   Relabeled For A Cause   27

4   Finding Your Calling   31

5   Bread . . . It's About The Process   39

6   The Why Behind Your What   48

7   Leave Your Luggage Behind   54

8   More Than: You Are A Lion, Not a Poodle   62

    Adequacy: A Special Note from Vonae   68

    About The Author   73

"IT'S YOU, BETHLEHEM,
IN JUDAH'S LAND,
NO LONGER BRINGING UP THE REAR.
FROM YOU WILL COME THE LEADER
WHO WILL SHEPHERD-RULE MY PEOPLE,
MY ISRAEL."

Chapter 1

IT ALL STARTS
WITH IDENTITY

Who Am I?

I'd never thought about my identity much before that fateful day. I was just Vonae, the second of four children, not the first girl, the desired boy, or the doted on baby girl.

Nope, just Vonae . . .

The seemingly black sheep of the family who was jokingly and lovingly referred to as the hobbit. I inherited that name due to my preference for being alone. I would get lost in the world of words, spending hours reading curled up in my bedroom or lost in the words of my journal. I didn't and still don't for that matter talk much, which drives my parents crazy. I'm a listener, people watcher, reader, learner, and at that time a seventh grade middle school student.

Not just any middle schooler, oh no, I was *the* middle schooler.

In those days, I appeared to have it all. The popularity, coveted cheerleading uniform, boyfriends (albeit too many), best friends and the list could continue, but if we're being honest, I still felt invisible and alone.

Well, invisible until the day my entire world was flipped upside down like an hour glass; each tiny piece of sand slithering through the constricted center, bringing me closer and closer to a nervous breakdown.

On that normal day in May of 2000, I watched as my beloved teacher was slain before me by a person I trusted, a person I laughed with, a person I had called friend. The sound of the gun radiated through the air as my teacher, mentor and friend fell to the ground. I grasped for understanding in the midst of chaos, students screaming, wailing, running and pushing; all of them trying to get somewhere, anywhere, but there. The classroom where they once found confidence, pride and acceptance was now a place of terror, confusion and devastation. Frozen in place, I pleaded for my teacher to get up from the floor, but he didn't move.

At that moment, that quick instant in an everlasting eternity, my identity seemed to have been branded in stone. I became the Lake Worth Middle girl.

It baffles me how effectively our past can haunt us. One wrong word can be the nail that closes a coffin on a friendship. One bad choice on a drunken night can result in a broken home. One spontaneous decision to chase love instead of investing in our future can leave us grappling for purpose and our dreams. Will we ever become who we imagined we'd be? Will we forever be marked and marred by our past mistakes, decisions and shortcomings?

It has been over ten years since that dark day in May and along the way, I've collected quite a few labels.

Snob. Murderer. Mean Girl. Snitch. Ugly. Imperfect. Popular. That girl. Most likely to succeed. Important. College student. Writer. Teacher. Wife. Mother. Failure. Inadequate. Insufficient. Unqualified. Unwanted.

Some of those I wore like a badge of honor. I was proud to be this or that. It was who I was. What defined me. What I could point to as if to say, "See, this is why I'm important. Can't you see what I've accomplished? Can't you see how hard I've worked? Here are all my accolades."

The funny thing about labels is that most of them come from other people- our parents, teachers, friends, classmates, colleagues, bosses, professors, boyfriends, husbands and children. These labels have the power to build us up or knock us down.

Taking a look back at my first list, there are a few positives, but the ones I can recall the clearest are the negatives. The ones that cut so deep that it hurt, keeping me imprisoned in insecurity and inadequacy. Negative words spoken into our lives are like a vine, slowly creeping in, growing, expanding and entangling us until they're finally able to choke the life and dreams out.

The word failure, a self-inflicted label, was enough to keep me from moving forward with any aspirations. After college, I had a grand plan. I would move to Los Angeles, write Young Adult novels, screenplays and television shows with the intention of becoming a famed movie producer. I would stomp around in my Christian Louboutin's and designer threads while sipping on my favorite Starbucks drink and jumping into my Maserati convertible.

And then reality hit.
It always does, doesn't it?

While I did acquire bits and pieces of that plan, all the other missed marks amounted to failure in my mind. Instead of living the dream, I settled. Settled for the opportunity to become a teacher, moving back to West Palm Beach to "figure things out." Now there's nothing wrong with being a teacher, absolutely nothing. I loved my students dearly and still communicate with many of them, but in my young mind, I was a failure.

I was devastated as I packed up my college apartment and headed south from Orlando. Never in my plans of life would Palm Beach County have been written in. It's safe to say that in that particular season of my life, I despised it. I despised the fact that there were no seasons, just hot, hot and semi-hot; the only place where people whip out their winter scarves when it happens to dip below eighty degrees. For me, being back in Palm Beach County meant that I had not made it, that I wouldn't achieve my dreams (ever) and most glaringly, that I was a failure.

I immersed myself into being an educator, rising in the ranks until I became lead teacher with the intentions of becoming an administrator. I was sought after, respected, wanted, well compensated and loved. Once again, I had found significance. I was a teacher, a sixth grade "lead" English teacher to be exact. I had finally made something of myself, but why did I still feel so empty?

According to the world's standards, I had it all; the fancy car, home, salary, husband, exquisite dinners, etc. But when I took a step back and looked at everything I had attained, all those things amounted to nothing. I felt confined by my celebrated label, windowless classroom, never ending lesson plans, six period days and the nature of a set daily routine.

While I had it all, life was mundane, predictable and unfulfilling.

As I desired to have more and do more, I realized that a life of fulfillment had nothing to do with a label. I wanted more than a label; I wanted significance. I desired to help my students by becoming a teacher who cared about their needs, not a standardized test or what I could attain.

Setting out, I had no idea what that would look like, so I began the only place I knew how: their bellies. I headed out to the local wholesaler, hubby in tow, and filled our cart with breakfast items, chips, cookies, candy and all sorts of other goodies. It was my naive attempt at making each student feel valued, but like any other poorly thought out plan, it didn't seem to be enough. Although they loved the idea of being rewarded for hard work, the results weren't exactly what I was aiming for. I wanted to change their lives, their character and their hearts.

The following year, I felt the call to start an afterschool program for teenage girls that would teach them leadership and etiquette skills, while showing them the importance of academics and setting goals for themselves. Once again, I buried myself in writing curriculum, building an organization and planning fun activities and serving opportunities for the enrolled students.

And just like that, I was back on top, receiving the accolades from my peers, parents of students, community leaders and co-workers. Organizations sought me out to see and hear what I had to offer. My schools administration praised my hard work and ability to streamline students who had serious behavioral issues. Everything was going so well. I was soaring fast to the top, patting myself on the back, basking in the accolades, feeling the glory of having position until, in what seemed like an instance, everything was gone.

A Label Removed

Have you ever felt called to leave your career and step fully into your passion or desires? It's like you're slowly being drawn out and disconnected from everything it involves. All of a sudden, you're standing on the edge of a metaphorical cliff, staring down into the great abyss. You can stay there in the contentment, or you can take a leap into the unknown, challenging yourself and trusting in a greater purpose.

That's exactly where I found myself. Teetering on the edge of that cliff, not knowing how in the world I could leave my career and still survive. The day I gave my resignation was filled with mixed emotions; fear, anxiety, trust, excitement and best of all, the freedom to start dreaming again. Oh, to be free. As strange as it may sound, after quitting my job and jumping into the unknown, it was like the whole world opened up to me. I was free to explore, create, write and finally live. Little did I know, that one step of faith would lead me into a season of great change, humbling and repurposing.

As I reflect on 2012, the dark and gloomy presence of that year makes me shudder. If we're being honest, which I hope we are, the only good thing that came out of that year was my son. Or so I thought.

Have you ever had a season like that?
Bless your heart for surviving.

You see, not only was that the year I resigned from my promising career, it was also the time that I stepped out of leadership in my church, being confined to my home due to motion sickness. Just the mere thought of having to drive somewhere made my stomach twists into a thousand knots. To describe my demeanor as an angry, crazy, pregnant woman would be a vast understatement. I didn't want to talk to anyone, be bothered by anyone, and I certainly didn't want to help anyone. To put it as plain as I can, I was a big giant mess. A big mess that felt sorry for herself and everything I gave up to "dream."

In one swift swoop, every bit of significance I could hold onto was gone. I didn't have this title to point to, or that accolade to boast about. All my labels had been removed. There was nothing left, just me and a glimpse of my would be dreams.

But this isn't just about me.
It's about you too.

What are some labels you wear or have worn like a badge, only to have them ripped away unexpectedly? Mom? Daughter? Girlfriend? Wife? Sister? Friend? President? Executive? Homemaker?

I'm going to give you some time to reflect on your labels or past labels removed. As they come to mind, list them in the space provided below.

_____
_____
_____
_____

Look at those labels, take them in, savor them and now prepare to reflect.

What were the hard lessons you had to learn in those seasons of life? Are learning at this very moment?

_____
_____
_____
_____
_____

If there's one thing I know is true, is that when there's nothing left to point to, boast about, or be proud of, the only thing that is left is you and God. In that deep dark time, I pleaded with Him for an answer. Why did I deserve such treatment? Why was He letting this happen to me? What had I done to have everything ripped away? Little did I know, my label wasn't being removed because of something I had done and yours may not have been either.

How easy is it for us to curl up into a ball and sulk? Wondering what on Earth we did to deserve such treatment, such torture, that leaves us scathed and feeling like nobodies. It's shocking how tightly we hold onto the label acquired by our degree, marital status, social economical status, or child bearing. It's almost as if we forget that we are so much more than *that* thing we want so badly. So much so, that when it's taken from us, we literally have nothing.

And nothing hurts.

Nothing hurts so bad that we're forced to listen to what's inside. To dig around for potential, long forgotten dreams or whispered promises. Any glimmer of hope will do. Nothing humbles us, builds our character, or gives us time to invest into others quite like it. Most importantly, nothing makes us reflect on who we are, who we were and who we want to be.

When we become nothing, we are in the position to be molded into exactly who we were created to be.

Who are You?

Who are you?

Before you answer, I want you to think about it for a moment. There's a statistic that says you're a culmination of the five people closest to you. With that said, I ask again, who are you? Who would your friends, colleagues, family members or significant other say you are?

Would you agree?
More than likely, your answer is no.

Those on the outside tend to see what we project, our "public selves." You know, the best foot forward, engaging, most-likeable version of us. Even worse are those who are closest to you, the ones who have known you for years. Maybe they grew up with you and unfortunately no matter how hard you try, you'll always be *that* person.

There's a song by the artist Brandon Heath, called "I'm not who I was," that has become the anthem to my life and maybe the new one to yours as well. In the song, Brandon recounts all the old memories of who he once was, but then disclaims them by exclaiming, "I'm not who I was!" Can't help but love the attitude of someone determined to change, shed the old image and then refuse to let anyone re-associate them with a person they may not be anymore. Now I completely understand that we cannot hide from our past or shed who we once were, but we also don't have to let that define who we will always be.

So I ask again, who are you? Was your previous answer based on what someone else would have answered for you, something that they point to like a flashing marquee? What is your headlining description?

Mom? Wife? Single? Independent?

Divorced? Widowed? Hopeless? Damaged?
Successful? Unsuccessful? Teacher? Mistress? Girlfriend?

It's far too easy to allow others to define who we are. It's like giving an architect the bid to construct your dream home. You tell them what you want, your budget, the specs and expectations and they go to work laying out the plans. These detailed plans include the bedrooms, bathrooms, kitchen, dining room, and if you're lucky, a mancave that will keep all the guys off your good stuff. The reality is that if you're going to get the house of your dreams, it will take the effort of a skilled architect and many other individuals to make it a reality. Unlike building a home, we cannot bid out our identity to others.

Consider this: you are the most immaculate dream home you could ever dream up. The foundation on which you sit is your past. It is cemented into you. Family memories, old boyfriends, crushes, friendships, dates gone bad, dates gone good, high school, middle school (yuck) and the many odd jobs you wont actually admit to having. Since those pivotal years laid the groundwork of your character, they are the beginning block to what the rest of you, your house, will be built on.

As your house goes under construction, it must be framed out. These wooden beams are essential to the sturdiness and structure of the overall home. Yes, I remodel my home and watch HGTV way too much, but stick with me here. These beams represent the seasons of your life. They are the most dominant traits, lessons and or callings in your heart. It's what drives you forward, keeps you dreaming, gives you hope and hey since you're a theoretical house, keeps you standing. No matter what goes on the outside, whether you choose brick or stucco, make-up or all natural, career or service, those fundamental beams remain.

Now, take a moment and ponder that. Do you see them, those thick wooden beams standing tall and sturdy inside you? What do they look like? What are they supporting? Are they under pressure, loosely tied or rotting?

So finally, I ask . . .
Who are you?

Take some time in the space below to write it down, flush it out. Getting it all out there and down on paper is what makes it real. Be honest, we won't judge you.

I'll even go first.

1. Steadfast
2. Dreamer
3. Assertive
4. Confident
5. Easily Disappointed
6. Empathetic
7. Determined
8. Fearful

You see, not all of our beams offer sufficient support, but when we identify the faulty ones, we are able to lean on the stronger beams to help us keep growing and moving forward.

Before we move any further, fill these lines with who you are and hey, even who you want to be. Your future self is waiting.

_____

_____

_____

_____

_____

_____

_____

_____

Chapter 2

MAKE NO MISTAKE

Here for a Reason

Several Christmases ago, I received a beautiful silver bird pendant from a dear friend of mine with a wonderful quote by Emily Dickinson inscribed on it. I hung the soaring bird on my rearview mirror so that it would constantly remind me that "We never know how good we are, until we are called to rise."

Isn't that the truth?

For some reason, we can believe that we are worthless, unwanted or inadequate, but to believe the opposite takes a radical call up. A charge! An extreme dose of gumption for us to believe that we are good, that we can be better. Heck, that we can even be great!

Consider this book, this moment, your call to rise.

You see, we were all put on this Earth for a marvelous plan and purpose. I like to say that God doesn't waste time, and He certainly didn't waste time when He placed you on this Earth. You're here for a special time, purpose and calling.

Don't believe me?

Let me tell you a story about a family of three that I know. It consists of a mom, dad, and their sweet little baby boy. While on the outside they may look normal, the reality is that none of them were ever "planned" to grace this Earth with their presence. We'll start our journey with the story of the patriarch of the family.

His story starts in the heat of Egypt. The youngest of three children born to Egyptian parents, this father would have never existed had it not been for divine intervention through a freak accident. After two high-risk pregnancies, his mother was advised that she should not have any more children in fear that the next would produce less than favorable results for her own health and that of the child's. In short, it would either be her life or the unborn offspring's.

Upon finding out they were expecting once more, the family was devastated. What would they do? How would the mom survive yet another dangerous nine months? The joyous news was quickly shrouded by the dark reality; they would have no choice but to terminate the tiny baby that was growing inside the mother's womb.

As the day came to have the procedure, the parents boarded a crowded bus that would take them to downtown Cairo where the doctor's office was located. Due to the conditions of Egypt at that time, public transportation wasn't always the safest, but it was the fastest and most convenient. Being that there wasn't enough space to sit, the father had to hold onto the outside of the bus on a makeshift guardrail while his pregnant wife sat inside. I'm not sure if you have ever been to a country like Egypt, but picture a hot, packed, makeshift bus with people tumbling out of every which side.

Now picture a road filled to capacity with cars and vespas, all zooming too fast from lane to lane, barely missing large potholes from where the ground had buckled under enormous weight and usage.

As the bus journeyed towards its destination, the driver hit a pothole, sending the father tumbling off the bus, his leg getting crushed under the vehicle's tires. Realizing the magnitude of what had just happened, the wife along with other passengers rushed him to the hospital. Requiring surgery and time for full recovery, he ended up spending an extended amount of time in the hospital. Because of strict cultural customs at that time, women were unable to seek an abortion without the accompaniment of her husband. Thus, she missed her window of opportunity and our said father of this normal family of three was born.

The mom's story is a lot less eventful, having more to do with disobedience to a doctor's orders than an unforeseen injury. The mother of this family was conceived very shortly after a heartbreaking miscarriage. After carrying their much desired baby boy, the parents of the mom in our normal family experienced a devastating loss. After learning they wouldn't be proud parents of a bouncing baby boy, the doctor ended their visit with a senseless statement. "She's young, she can have another kid. Take her out and buy her some shoes." Like somehow a pair of shoes could suffice for the loss of a child.

In her grief, she was engulfed by the feeling of inadequacy in being able to carry a baby full term and the fear of even trying again, only to be devastated by yet another miscarriage. They were taken aback, blindsided by the possibility of not being able to have another child, but somewhere they found a glimmer of hope. Determined, they set out to try again, getting pregnant shortly after with a baby girl who would become the mother of this special little family of three.

Finally, there is the story of the precious little toddler boy; the one and a half year old who simply was never supposed to be. After getting married in November and enjoying the honeymoon phase of their first few months, the parents of this little one were shocked to find out they were expecting their first child. Heck, they had only been married for seven months. Were things supposed to work that fast? Not sure, but they certainly did. The "problem" they faced was that their lives were busy; things moved too fast, they were important, sought after, leaders of this and that. Where would a child fit into such an equation? They'd be the only one of their friends with a baby, not to mention married. Gasp! But her cycle was late and she knew what that meant.

Test number one came back positive, but that couldn't be true. There had to be some sort of a glitch. Twelve positive tests later, yes twelve, the reality set in. This pregnancy was going to happen so they'd better get over their previous parental disqualifiers. As much as she didn't want to admit it, she struggled with the truth that she was carrying a child. So much so, that she enlisted the assistance of a friend, begging her to take a test so that they could compare results. When the reality hit that her friend's test was in fact negative, she had to come to terms with the truth. She was pregnant.

Unfortunately, she didn't feel the burst of excitement or experience those first joyous moments of becoming a mom. All in all, to a twenty-four year old, the entire ordeal just seemed like a major inconvenience. An inconvenience that is, until one day when she went to work and the heavy flow started.

At first she was relieved, thinking that the whole pregnancy scare had to have just been a false alarm. But when things didn't lighten up all day and then were accompanied by jarring lightning bolts of pain shooting through her body, she knew something was wrong. One search on Google revealed what she would have never expected. She was having a miscarriage. The baby she wasn't quite convinced she wanted was being taken away from her; leaving in its place a huge hole in her heart and a hefty helping of guilt.

All of a sudden, those selfish ambitions meant nothing. The guilt of knowing that she hadn't appreciated the gift given until it was taken away was more than she could bear. Weeks passed and then months, as tears continued to stream down her face. The feelings of failure and loss consumed her until she was completely isolated in one of the darkest places of her life. Never would she try to have another child. The pain of another loss would be too much to handle. That was until one afternoon when her unsuspecting husband began eating her food and she responded by nearly tackling him to the ground. Not realizing her reaction until he and her sister (who she was on the telephone with at the time) both inquired if she was pregnant because of her over the top response to someone taking her food.

In an effort to humor them, she took a test. Unbeknownst to her, she was once again pregnant, completing the family of three. A family who each individually were never supposed to walk this Earth, but because they had a plan and a purpose, God plucked them out of eternity and placed them right here, right now.

Every time I ponder this story, my heart is filled with awe and wonder. For me, this story is a story of promise, of hope that I'm not just here for any old reason. That each breath I take, each person I meet and each season of life is culminating to a grand purpose and destiny. This story astounds me because it's the story of my small family of three. My husband who was supposed to be aborted, myself who simply shouldn't have been born, and my sweet little Jacob whose name means to supplant or come in place of. While we may not ever understand the details, heartbreaks and opportunities, everything that we experience is a tiny piece of a grand, marvelous plan.

Are you willing to live yours out with me?

The Plan

Have you ever felt like you have no idea what you're supposed to be doing with your life?
Where you're supposed to live?
Who you're supposed to marry?
How you ended up married to that guy? (That's a different book entirely.)
When your big break will come?
When will you get noticed?

Need I go on?
Nothing is more frustrating than having plans and then watching as none of *those* plans come to fruition.

Take high school for example. Everyone has their plan of who or what they want to be when they grow up. Little do they know, once college starts and they're two years in, their major will have changed at least three times. It's a guarantee of life. You can bet a hundred bucks that every plan you set out to make will always vary from what you originally intended.

Why? Because our plans suck.

We purchase that large home, not thinking of what it will take to maintain it, only to realize we didn't need it after all. We take that job making six figures because our plan requires it, but we barely have time to see our family or have a personal life outside of it. Our plans tend to be based on the grandiose of things, living to achieve the "American Dream."

But what if there's more to life, more to the plan prepared for us than that?

On the way to work the other day, I noticed a billboard with a shiny red Porsche displayed on it. The Porsche was pictured racing up the highway, gleaming in the sun as the rays hit its perfectly waxed paint. The marketing tagline read, "You have arrived." That was it, plain and simple. I don't know how many hundreds of thousands of people passed by that same billboard daily, but how disappointing would life be if all we were here for was to acquire stuff? To receive our dream car, house, career, financial status, relationship and then poof, our lives would be complete?

That seems unexcitingly depressing to me.

Now I'm not saying that we should not have nice cars or things. My small family of three is full of self-proclaimed car fiends. We literally live and breath fine pieces of well crafted machinery. Heck, my Jacob even wakes up, stands up in his crib and instead of saying mommy or daddy, shouts "car!" Yes son, good morning to you too.

The point is, the plan we were placed on this Earth for goes way beyond our needs and wants. It's an intricate masterpiece that weaves us together with another life and then with another until the impact is manifested into something beautiful. Something that will change lives, a generation, a government, a people and this world.

I love this quote:
"I know what I'm doing.
I have it all planned out-
plans to take care of you,
not abandon you,
plans to give you the future you hope for."
–The Message

Aren't you glad someone knows what's going on?

Think of the plan for your life as a jigsaw puzzle. One of those ones with a billion pieces that you start, get a migraine and then decide you'll finish some other time. Each season of your life fills a bit of that puzzle, pushing you towards your destiny. When you take one step forward, pieces are added, revealing more of the picture of your calling and destiny.

But if we're honest, sometimes we can get stuck on a section, searching and searching to find the piece that's missing. Something just isn't fitting. That's when we know there's something along the way that we've missed. Maybe it's a relationship we need to end or reconcile, a character flaw that needs to be worked out, a habit that's hindering us, or maybe a job we're being called out of. Can you see the missing puzzle piece? What is it that's keeping your current section from being completed?

_____
_____
_____
_____

Is your missing piece huge and looming, or just a pesky thing you want to hold onto? My hope is that you'll lay it down so you can see the unexpected happen in your life as the pieces of your puzzle continue to fall into place. The vibrant colors, memories, picturesque scenes that will make up your jigsaw masterpiece will be brilliant.

I'm so excited for you.

Can you imagine the wonder of what the plan for your life could be or the lives you could touch? The people you could be apart of saving, feeding, loving, inspiring, if only you could let that piece go and fill this season of your life? The possibilities of what you can experience are endless. You just have to make the choice to want it enough not to get stuck in the past or the here and now.

I love this quote from speaker Christine Caine:
"Courageous people step into the unknown, unexplored,

unchartered, uncomfortable, unpredictable, untapped, uncertain, unrevealed and undisclosed."

You may not be feeling all that courageous as you read these words, but I'm hoping a fire will be ignited in your heart. That your desire and dreams to go *there*, would far exceed your comfort in staying *here*.

In my everyday line of work, I have the privilege of listening and learning from people who are so much further in their journey of life than me. They're wiser, more organized and creative, and just so awe inspiring. Whenever I get the chance, I love to let them pour out their wisdom into my life. I'm intentional about internalizing every conversation and then as weeks pass, I ponder their words, strategically applying them to my life.

During one of these meetings, I happened to be doing what I love to do on any given Sunday, stuff my face with yummy breakfast items. As I attempted to scour the internet, eat some goodies and unlike my normal self (I promise), avoid conversation in an effort to get work done, one of those extraordinarily inspiring people came and sat in front of me. We talked for quite some time about the wonders of life. Well, let's be honest, I rambled some foolishness, he actually talked. What he said in those moments has been ringing in the chambers of my heart and mind ever since.

I had never heard his life's story or had the opportunity to glean from his wisdom prior to that chance encounter. As he sat there before me, he recounted his early days. The days of his youth when he dreamed wild, bold and courageous dreams; dreams of being a hero, joining the military, serving his country and traveling the world. As he ventured down that path, getting ever so close, something just didn't settle right within him. He felt this uneasy pang that maybe his deepest desire wasn't at all the plan that was marked out for his life. Instead, he felt his heart being directed towards missionary work.

Not knowing how to respond, how to navigate the absolute certainty that would accompany the military lifestyle- a guaranteed salary, housing and the chance to travel the world, he chose the latter. Instead of following the plan he had set for his life, he listened to the voice deep within his heart. The voice that whispered, "I have a special plan and future in store for you. Wont you just trust me? Be courageous."

And that's what he did.

Placing his plans aside for one's bigger than himself, he gained respect, honor and the utmost admiration from all those who have had the privilege of coming into contact with him. Not only did his dreams of traveling the world come true, he's been able to visit over one hundred and eighty countries. He'll be the first to admit that it wasn't because of anything he could have planned. It's only because he chose to be courageous, stepping into the unknown in order to embrace his calling.

Before we move on, I want you to take a moment and write down the plan you have for your life. What does it entail? Who does it include? Where would you like to go and/or end up? Why?

_____
_____
_____
_____
_____
_____
_____
_____
_____

A Purpose

Purpose.

What does it mean to have a purpose, to live with purpose or to act with purpose? To be purposeful in our pursuit of life is to strive for something beyond ourselves. I did a little digging (thanks Google) and it can be described as this:

1. The reason for which something is done or created or for which something exists.
2. To have as one's intention or objective.

I love that.

If we combine the two, we end up with the reason something was created and or intended for. You my friend were intended to do something great, to achieve a wonderful purpose and to exist right now in this moment, in order to do something beyond yourself. Remember the plan you wrote on the previous page? I want you to go back to it, pick it apart, dream bigger and most importantly think beyond yourself. On the following lines, write what comes from your heart, not your head. Forget about the material achievements, the fact that you'll have to earn a living and your potential status. In fact, there's a quote I hear quite often that says, "If you have food in the refrigerator, clothes on your back, a roof over your head and a place to sleep, you are richer than seventy-five percent of the world."

With that considered, we could all use a bit of a reality check, but let's get back on track. What is the one thing or things that tug at your heart when you see and/or hear about it? Is it human trafficking, childhood poverty, animals, homelessness, teenage suicide . . .

If you could go beyond yourself, what burden would you want to lift, fight for or conquer?

_____

_____

_____

_____

_____

_____

Whatever you wrote on those lines could very well be your purpose. It doesn't matter how big or small the task before you might be, as long as you're willing to be a small part of making a difference in the here and now.

A purpose doesn't have to be about conquering the world. It doesn't have to be some grand elaborate plan as long as your heart is in it. The key to living out your purpose is to start small. No one is able to doing something great in their life until they have done a slew of small menial things. It's the small steps that position you for the great adventure.

So where will you start?

One thing I've learned on this journey for purpose (yes, it is a journey) is that once I step into one thing, completing one small task (with the right attitude of course), my purpose tends to expand; to bend, flex and shift. The good thing about purpose is that the goal or overarching theme is always the same. It is the *how* in that purpose that will change as you are directed to live it out in each new season of your life.

At a young age, I felt this innate need to unify women. To create a place where they could belong, where they could be inspired and most pressing, where they could be empowered. A place where they could learn together and from each other, while doing fun and meaningful projects. When I was five that was in the form of a girl's club that my sister and I started in our parents' kitchen, membership dues and all. (We were young businesswomen.) In high school, that took the form of a young lady's social club affectionately dubbed Zeta Delta Sigma with the tagline, "Beauty of a rose, attitude of a thorn." (School administrators didn't take too kindly to that.) In college, after choosing to quit pledging a sorority who weren't at all who they said they were, I founded one named Psi Delta Epsilon; an organization whose goal was to simply give women purpose and meaning.

I didn't know it then, but each of those ideas, groups and organizations were driven by the purpose for my life. I may have felt like I failed at each one, but in those moments, for those girls, teens and ladies, they were filled with hope, trust, meaning and the assurance that they were believed in. No matter the outcome in those brief moments together, their lives were changed.

After college, I felt like that purpose had changed. That no longer was I to focus on women, but on the youth of the next generation. I started LEAD Youth Initiative, abandoning any hope of uniting or empowering women ever again. But what I didn't know was that this wasn't a call to abandonment, it was simply my purpose shifting, making room for more impact that would include a forgotten generation. A generation of children with absent parents, left to be raised by culture and what they learn on television.

With that new knowledge, I set out on a mission to teach leadership, etiquette skills, manners, dedication, determination and goal setting to a group of fifteen preteen girls. We laughed, cried, learned and served over our course of a year together. What first seemed like a purpose removed became one of the most fulfilling seasons of my life. Those girls may have learned from me, but I learned a lot more from them. Once again, without knowing it or even trying, I was instilling hope, courage and inspiration into women. I have come to realize that it doesn't matter the age of the recipient; your purpose will be fulfilled wherever God intends to use your gifts.

That brings us to today. Today I have the joys of knowing my purpose. Of following that purpose and trying my best to live it out everyday. As I write to you, I may not have the job I want, the salary I would like or the car I could only dream of, but I'm okay with that because I have never felt more fulfilled in my entire life.

My hope is that you would know without any doubt in your mind how badly I want you to find your purpose; to be able to step out beyond yourself and see the need in others, to know how blessed you are that you cant help but want to give to others. It's in the moments when we step outside of ourselves that we truly discover our intended purpose for walking this Earth.

You may be thinking that's all well and good, Vonae, but not everyone has an innate sense of what they're supposed to be doing. To that, I would say, you are correct. Sometimes our purpose is discovered through trials, hardships or personal tragedy. If you're reading this right now and you can identify, I hope you know you are dear and close to my heart. I know all too well what it feels like to face loss and devastation. To feel alone and broken with no sense of hope beyond the horizon, but remain confident that God will never give you more than you can handle. There's a lyric from a song by Brit Nicole that echoes that very sentiment:

Even when you cant imagine how,
How you ever gonna find your way out.
Even when you're drowning in your doubt,
Just look beyond the clouds.

No matter what you are facing right now, your purpose is greater that that. This trial will not destroy you unless you let it. This tragedy won't break your spirit, unless you give it permission to. I have seen some of the greatest, most passion driven purposes come out of moments of unexplainable tragedy. It's in the instant when you're heading down one path to a likely destination, only to be blindsided by the unthinkable, the unexplainable. I don't know if it was a bad diagnosis, the death of a loved one, the loss of a child, infidelity, a divorce, loss of finances or some other terrible unforeseen circumstance, but there is a God who is greater than all those things. A God who can take what seems like a mess in your life and turn it into a beautiful story of purpose, future and hope.

Don't believe me? Hopefully this will change your mind.

There is a hilarious and spunky television personality that I have followed for years. First on my college obsession E! News (I know, don't judge me) and then more recently on her reality show with her husband. For some reason, I find the two of them intriguing and entertaining; her with an extra helping of quirkiness and him with his down to Earth, stark reality checks. Maybe it's because they remind me a lot of my hubby and I. (I'll let you decide who the quirky one is.) As I followed their story, she shared openly about her struggles to conceive and the loss of a child through miscarriage as well as failed attempts at IVF. Did she know at the time that these trials could be reshaping her life and purpose? I highly doubt it, but how many women is she able to help through that particular journey now; to stand alongside them and provide comfort, encouragement and offer some sense of hope?

As the season of the show continued, they decided to take a year break that they dubbed the "year of fun." In that year, they did just that, had fun without worrying about their current circumstances. But as the year drew to a close, she wanted to try again. So they did. The only difference this time was that she would have to receive a mammogram in order to undergo another round of IVF. Something that seemed so innocent, so simple, would reveal devastating results. If you know the story, she found out that she had breast cancer. There's nothing like the C word to turn your world upside down. Understandably, she was shaken, bewildered and broken, but chose to be strong and courageous through her personal trials. From those moments, it seems like she's gained a new purpose, partnering with an organization to start an initiative that would grant wishes to women who have survived breast or ovarian cancer.

While the trial and storm she was in could have consumed her, she decided to share her story and struggles, and then harness the passion to champion a cause greater than herself.

The purposes for our lives come in all different shapes and sizes. Some are born and ingrained in us, while others just simply smack us in the face. No matter how your purpose comes to you, be courageous and willing to accept it with arms wide open.

Someone is waiting on you.

Chapter 3

✻

RELABELED FOR A CAUSE

"Our identity and purpose waits for us in the light." –Tom Mullins

I'm so happy that you've stayed on this journey with me. When we make the choice to be courageous, step beyond ourselves and embrace our purpose, our lives reach a pivotal turning point.

This is that turning point for you.
For me.

When we abandon our labels, reach beyond ourselves, and allow each part of us to be stretched and molded, something beautiful happens. We step out of the dark place of our life. A place we didn't realize wasn't our best, our purpose, our calling until we discover our new meaning for living, for existing. It's like we step into a bright, glimmering promise, a promise of purpose and cause. No longer are we concerned about what we can achieve. It becomes all about what we can give, who we can help and the amount of hope we can spread.

In the darkest moment of my life when I felt absolutely worthless, I had no idea I was being repositioned. That I would be giving up one label (teacher, leader, important) to put on a new more fulfilling label. In essence, I was stepping up and out of my dark place. A place where I worked extremely hard, made things happen, went, went and went some more until I fell down exhausted. Here's the scary and dangerous part: I knew there was so much more to life than my current situation; this incessant need to please others and amount to something, but I had no idea I was living in a dark place. A place that was so comfortable that I nearly missed my opportunity. The opportunity to be introduced to my calling and then step into the light.

The quote at the beginning of the chapter by Coach Tom Mullins says it all. Our purpose and calling waits for us in the light. It is there that we are relabeled for a cause. A cause so great, that the thought of us even being considered for such an honor is humbling. If there's one thing I can tell you, it's that a good humbling season can be a great thing.

When we take on our new label, a label filled with hope, life and mission, we have a confidence that we can achieve all that we were created to be. I don't know what labels you wrote down leading up to this chapter, but aren't you so glad to have the opportunity to shed them? Just like a butterfly does when it's shedding its cocoon in order to reveal a stunning wingspan. One that is intricate in design, delicate and graceful. You my friend, have been made new.

Instead of being unwanted, you have been chosen.
Instead of being a failure, you are victorious.
Even more than that, you are beautiful, intelligent, wanted, accepted, joyful, loved, desired, unique and set apart.

You are more than any word that I could ever put on this page, because you were crafted in His image and He adores you.

He's just waiting. They're waiting. Waiting for you to step out in faith and take hold of your purpose, to take hold of your destiny. You see, when everything is gone and a new label is affixed, it's like a fresh breath of air has been pumped into your lungs. A crisp, spring wind that blows among the newly budded flowers, dancing along a lightly dewed blade of grass before caressing our face on its way to breathe new life.

You can have the promise of new life.

As you've quieted yourself and reflected through the pages of this book, what is the one word that has replaced all the noise in your life?

The one new label that you can hold onto as you step into this new season? _____

That word, as simple as it may be, serves as the driving point to your destiny. In order to be relabeled and stay that way, that word needs to be affixed in your mind, engraved in your heart and most of all, believed by you. Like every season, the word may change. It just means you've embraced that label, internalized it and now it can be replaced with a new affirmation.

When I first began to feel God relabeling me for a cause, I fought hard against it. I simply couldn't believe that I could become those things. But something began to happen as I wrote them, spoke them, imagined them and then slowly believed them. All of a sudden, something that seemed dead, impossible even, began to come alive. Slowly, I felt chosen. (My first word.) No longer did the words or reactions from other people questioning my ability or qualifications to do or try something matter to me. I didn't have to shrink back or cower because I was chosen; Chosen of God, by God and for God.

Now I'll be the first to admit that your relabeling and walking out that label may not go over well with those around you. What do I mean? I'm so glad you asked. For some time, I've had the privilege to serve with a talented gentleman who loves to offer his take on things. Not just on work related things, nope those would be sufficient enough, he offers it on almost everything. As the months passed and things picked up and then slowed down again, he turned to me and said, "I'm so glad you have this position. I wasn't sure about you in the beginning, but you really belong here."

Just to give you a little back-story, this has been a place where I've had the privilege to serve a while. A position that I didn't go after, apply for, or seek out. It was one of those things that just so happened to fall into my lap. It may sound kooky, but I was "chosen" for it. It was almost as if God wanted to let me know that He had not forgotten about His promises or me, so plop right into my lap came this new position. Immediately, I felt overwhelmed and unqualified. There were two other candidates who I'm sure had degrees in seminary and theology to one up my degree in English. I mean seriously, it didn't get anymore unqualified than me. But among all the doubt and fear (not to mention someone actually telling me "You're not qualified for this job," yeah that really happened) the word chosen kept playing in my mind. As I made that my mantra, it no longer mattered what my degree or qualifications said about me. I began to focus on what God said about me.

As I stood there, shocked at his realization that I should have the position I've been blessed to hold, I just smiled. Knowing that I was chosen to do what I get to do; that outweighs the approval or affirmation of anyone any day.

So as I set out to remain chosen, I had to fix my gaze on Him. The one who had called me and gave me a promise of a future, and that's what you'll have to do as well. As you shift and flex through different seasons and labels, I want to challenge you to hold tightly to them. To not let anyone else discredit the word God has spoken into your heart. Each word is a stepping stone to the next season of your life, but you must be willing to embrace it and then step into your future.

Chapter 4

FINDING YOUR CALLING

Every Wednesday I have the opportunity to meet with some lovely young ladies and help them navigate life. The conversations can range from joyous laughter, extreme disappointment and flat out uncertainty. Needless to say, Wednesday has become one of my favorite days of the week.

Before you write me off as a creeper, it's not because I have some sick obsession with other people's issues. I have enough problems of my own to last me a lifetime. I enjoy it so much because I know it's apart of my calling; that they are apart of my calling. And when you start living in your calling, there is absolutely nothing else like it.

The other day, as I sat having one of those conversations,

my dear friend expressed her desire to quit her job and ministry completely. For someone like me who wants everyone to live a great life of purpose, it was like a dagger to my heart. Why? Because I didn't want her to jump ship before discovering the reason she was in her current position and career. Would her quitting impact me directly? No, not at all, but I'm a strong believer in learning something from every season and place we find ourselves in.

So, I set out to do what I do best, play devil's advocate. Asking her question after question, I tried desperately to make her see the importance of learning from every situation. Even if she absolutely hated her job and boss, there was something to be learned. Right?

Well, after a while, she finally just asked, "How do I know what my calling is?"

That question stopped me right in my tracks. I had never thought about it before. It was my assumption that everyone knew his or her calling. That we all had some inkling deep down of just what we were placed on this Earth to do, but clearly that was not the case. Maybe you're in the same boat as her, wondering the same exact thing. What is a calling and how do I know I'm walking in mine? Or simply, where the heck do you find your calling?

As I pondered her question, I racked my brain for the very place that I first realized my calling. It wasn't a lightning strike out of the sky moment, although I'm sure that does happen. The revelation of my calling came piece by piece as God placed little desires, ideas, and dreams in my heart; positioning me for opportunities that I would have never thought were possible.

To put it simply, your calling starts with one tiny seed.

The seed that propels you into your calling is an initial act or engagement. It's the intentional involvement in an activity, volunteer event, or situation. *Intentional* being the key word. Callings aren't found sitting at home hoping, dreaming and wishing that you'll figure yours out. It's about getting out there, getting involved and being vulnerable.

The first seed of my life was planted way back in high school, but I didn't know it then. Time and time again, I found myself creating places for women to connect, grow and be in community. As I graduated college, I found myself wanting less of sorority life and more of a place of accountability and growth. So what did I do? I sought out a women's life group. I became intentional about that growth and what it would mean for me to step out as a woman of faith into a group of other women I didn't even know.

I remember that first meeting vividly. All the women present appeared so well established, well versed and put together. It seemed like each girl sported the finest clothes from the likes of Anthropologie, not to mention the giant sparklers on *that* finger. Who was I, just some girl off the street looking to get involved? A girl without a clue where she belonged or who she was but that was okay, because these girls would be the starting point of who I was supposed to be.

After that first meeting, I was entranced. Finally, I didn't have to do life alone. There was a network of powerful women standing right beside me, cheering me on, calling me up and telling me who I was going to be; although at the time I thought they were absolutely nuts! Those same ladies are still doing great things and I admire each and every one of them for it. As the weeks continued, my heart began to fill with hope and determination to reach out to ladies who didn't have the type of support system I did. I became an advocate for community and inclusiveness. If only we could make every woman who walked through our doors feel special, oh, how we could change the world.

And that's when my calling began to take shape.

It was a regular Fall evening when the leader of our women's group announced that she would no longer be able to continue leading. We were all shocked and emotion ran high. What would it look like for us now if she left? She was our inspiration; the model of a woman we all sought to emulate, and now she was stepping down.

What on Earth were we supposed to do?

Going home that night, I was devastated to say the least. Was I supposed to go find another group, or fade back into oblivion? Pondering my next step, I felt a tiny inkling in my heart offer up an answer; I was supposed to begin leading the group.

Wait . . .
What? Me? There was no way!

The doubts in my mind started immediately but just as they entered, I texted our leader to get her thoughts and to my dismay, she confirmed what the inkling was telling me. I was in fact supposed to lead the group.

I was terrified.
She was delighted.

As we step out into a vulnerable place, a seed is planted into our hearts. In order for that seed, or any seed for that matter, to develop any further, it has to be planted in fertile soil and then watered consistently. The fertile soil is a place of positivity, inspiration and growth, while the water serves as the outside opportunities that lead us closer to our next step. Without the watering, it doesn't matter how great the soil is;

the seed will never have what it needs to sprout. The environment in which we intentionally place ourselves becomes the soil for our calling and the opportunities (water) are what challenge us to sprout.

So, there I was. Perfectly positioned to inspire ladies as I grew in my own personal faith. The soil was rich and I lavished the community that was built with these ladies. People came and went. There were good seasons and bad seasons. Conflict to navigate, births to celebrate and relocations to mourn, but as each of these situations watered the initial seed, I began to realize that the person I was when we first started, looked drastically different from who I had become. I was confident, strong and sure of who I was. No longer was I the girl from the outside. I had fully embraced this new season and was now the woman others looked to for inspiration and direction.

I had put down roots.

The roots of our calling begin to occupy space when we have an understanding of what that calling may be. We can't see the big picture and have no idea where we're headed, but we begin to feel value and an assurance that *this* is what we were made for.

This is what we've been looking for.

Putting down roots is such a crucial part of your journey. As I type this, my heart is overwhelmed with excitement for you as you begin to sprout and put down roots. So much so, that I'm going to just be quiet. Give you a moment to reflect and ponder.

What situations and/or opportunities have served as watering moments for you?

_____
_____
_____
_____
_____
_____
_____
_____

As you allow yourself to be watered, stretched and grown, how have your roots expanded, strengthened?

_____
_____
_____
_____
_____
_____
_____
_____

What was or has been a seed in your life? Have you nourished that seed or abandoned it?

_____
_____
_____
_____
_____
_____
_____
_____

Was that enough silence?

Good, because we're going to tackle some more, but first let's address the topic of an abandoned seed. I don't know if you put abandoned or not, but I feel like someone needs to hear this even if it's one lady out of a million.

Just because you abandoned a seed, doesn't mean all hope is lost. Your life is not over and your chance to live out your calling hasn't been revoked. It is never too late for us to start living out our calling, to step into the grand purpose for our life and see immense transformation and personal satisfaction come. We just have to be willing to start again. Will you start again? For your sake and for the sake of those waiting for you, I hope so.

Now that we've covered that, let's move on.

A seed doesn't start putting down roots unless it's sure the soil it is planted in is able to sustain it. Likewise, if you find yourself in a situation that is unhealthy and not at all what you think you should be doing, it's okay to start again. It's better to be a rose planted in a solitary pot than one who is planted in a place occupied by weeds. Weeds are the people, things and circumstances that choke out your dreams. They criticize, ostracize and break you down until there is literally nothing left.

In my backyard I have three rose bushes, all of which have been gifted to me by my wonderful father-in-law. I've said it before, but I'll say it again, I'm not exactly Susie Homemaker; probably as far away from her as humanly possible. Although I'm not domestically savvy and am a professional at killing plants (even the most self-sustaining) I've always had this dream of having a beautiful rose garden. You know, like the one from The Secret Garden? I love big beautiful blooms, but would love them more if I could keep them alive.

Anyhow, as last year progressed and work became extremely busy, I began to neglect my little space of serenity in the backyard.

Weeds moved in, blossomed and quickly consumed it's inhabitants. I don't know how long the weeds had the opportunity to grow, I would say more than six months, before I finally ventured into the backyard and saw that two of the three rose bushes had been choked nearly to death.

I was devastated and more, terrified of what my father-in-law would say if he saw this catastrophe. The one plant that seemed to be holding on and sustaining the best was the one with deep roots. The other two that I had received months before withered and all but disappeared.

What an identical picture of what happens in our lives.

We plant ourselves in an area that we think is great and healthy for thriving, but then we neglect what it takes to keep us growing. We allow the weeds of our lives to occupy space, choking out our hope, aspirations and drive. It wasn't the plants' fault they were dying. It was mine. I allowed my surroundings to keep me so busy that I began to neglect what I held valuable.

The same goes for others and the soil we choose to plant ourselves in. It's not their faults the life is getting choked out of us. In fact, when we allow weeds to come in and take up residence, we're giving them permission to dictate our lives and future. A weed can only borough as deep as you will let it. So be proactive and do a little weeding in your life.

Once you've cleaned up, dig in your roots and start to realize who you are. Our callings are largely based on who we have already been. Those past situations become our story; the way that we relate to others and invite them into our world. As we merge our past with the present, something magnificent begins to grow. No longer are we bound by our past regrets and shameful acts. They become the base of all we will ever do or accomplish. They are the very things that we stand on to elevate us and propel us forward. We all of a sudden realize that what we have overcome we can use to help someone else overcome. And before we know it, no longer are we operating as a seed. No, we are the fully blossomed version of who we were always meant to be. We realize that finally we are living in our calling. It may not be easy to recognize at first, but one day you'll look around, gasp, and know this is exactly what you were created to do.

Chapter 5

BREAD . . .
IT'S ALL ABOUT THE PROCESS

You may be wondering what bread has to do with anything.
What do you mean?
It has to do with everything!

Well not really, but the process of making bread has everything to do with getting from our calling to walking in our promised land; the place where we live in abundance and fulfillment.

Wait . . .

Did I really just say process? Am I telling you that you wont just find your calling and then poof, start living it out instantly?

Well, yes.

That's exactly what I'm telling you. How do I know? I know this because God doesn't call us into something that He hasn't been preparing us for. If He did, we wouldn't last a year in that purpose. So instead, he takes us on a refining process. A process that looks a lot like making bread.

Before we get into that process, let's take a little side step. I don't know about you, but when I finally figure out my calling, I want to live it now! I don't want to have to wait on the sidelines watching everyone else achieve, receive accolades and enjoy living their lives of fulfillment. I'm apart of the NOW generation.

I want it NOW!

How about you? Are you suffering from NOWrosis?

You can be honest. You're certainly not alone. As I've gone through my own preparation process, I can see now what I didn't see then. I can see the closed doors and the value that was in them. I can see the building of character and chipping away of a hardened heart. In short, I can see the beauty in the process as I wade waist deep through the Master's step-by-step recipe for success. And for your sake as well as mine, I'm thankful. I'm thankful that He cares enough about us to make us well and whole, over making us happy.

Now I have to admit, I'm not a huge fan of bread. Unlike my wonderful mother, who is for all intents and purposes, a bread connoisseur. I lean on the side of caution when it comes to taking in such a tempting treat. Mostly because of my sister's famous saying, "Bread makes you spread," or Christine Caine's mantra, "The whiter the bread the quicker your dead." Both scare me enough to keep my bread consumption to a minimum. Although, if you put a basket of Cheesecake Factory's brown pumpernickel bread in front of me, all bets are off!

So, let's get into the bread making process.

Imagine for a moment, you're standing in a pantry. This pantry is white, crisp and aligned with mahogany shelves. It's large in expanse, so much so, you could do a cartwheel if the mood strikes you. Draped from the ceiling is a beautiful crystal chandelier, that reflects off the many glass mason jars labeled just so. As you walk among the perfectly stocked shelves, you look at the list of items you need to make your award winning bread:

1. Flour
2. Yeast
3. Salt
4. Sugar
5. Milk
6. Shortening

That's it. Those are the key ingredients to your award winning bread. Well, maybe not, but let's go with it anyway. The process of God taking us from our calling to our promised land has to do with all the different ingredients of our lives and the stages that we pass through. Those stages end up looking a lot like the bread preparation process; the mixing, kneading and baking. Just like when you're making a loaf of bread, when we were each designed, there were key ingredients that were tossed into our bowls.

For instance, flour is the foundation of each of our lives. It's our childhood memories, adolescent years and young adult years. Just as flour is essential for making bread, so are each of the experiences we have throughout life, leading up until our moment of calling. As much as we may try to sift through the memories of life, shaking them off because of shame, regret or loss, each of those stories and situations are a part of us; a part of the story that will help us deliver someone who may very well be dealing with something now that we dealt with in the past.

Maybe a part of your story is abuse, rape, abortion, a miscarriage, loss, devastation, being unwanted, a mistake, abandoned, forgotten, mistreated, used and the list could go on. I know each of these on their own can be crippling and no doubt, they are. But to know that we are not alone, to know that there are others who are dealing with the same issue, the same hurt, the same devastation that we have already dealt with but have come out on the other side victorious gives us a story. It gives us a starting point and open door. The foundation of our past opens a wonderful door for the future. We are granted backstage access into someone's life when we can stand beside him or her and say, "I have been there. I have hurt that way." But more than just being able to relate, it opens the door for us to walk them down the path of restoring the life they should have always had, the life that was promised to them.

So don't sift your flour, it's the foundation of who you are.

Now, the next ingredients are my favorites, sugar and salt. It's so interesting to me as I imagine that large mixing bowl with a few cups of flour settled in, that some of us have a lot more of one ingredient than the other. I don't have to take a survey to know which one I received a good helping of. The resounding answer would be salt. I'm sure there's a bit of sugar somewhere in me, but I'm a lot spicier than I am sweet. When I think about these two ingredients, individual personality comes to mind. Each of us has been gifted with a specific personality. Contrary to what you may have heard from peers, your parents, teachers, friends or a loved one, the amount of sugar or salt you received was strategically planned.

If you're sweet and loving, there is a great reason for that. For some reason, you were given a few extra sprinkles of sugar. You just may be the one encouraging word that the woman walking down the street gets all week, all year. You may be the only teacher who ever hugs that young man and tells him he is special, smart, and talented, changing the trajectory of his life. The extra amount of sugar you've been given can be equated to the level of care, love and kindness you naturally extend to others. While most have to work at lending a helping hand, it is in your very design to be uplifting and nurturing. That is a very special trait that others (like me) have to work hard at achieving throughout their life. I would encourage you to hold onto and foster that. Don't go searching for more salt.

On the other hand, if you've received more salt in your recipe, than you know just how hard it can be to be caring and nurturing. The spicier you are, the more apt you could be to tell it like it is. You are willing to say the hard things, to make changes and to shake things up. While there's nothing wrong with having a little more salt in your bowl, it can equally be a challenge to make sure you're not simply being negative. Those with more salt tend to be the "counselors" among their peers, because they're known for their honesty and straightforwardness. While there is value in having an opinion, be careful not to allow your personality to become judgmental. It is equally important to guard your words, as it is to offer your opinion.

While there are some other ingredients mixed into the bread of life, the exciting factor that we all get a good heaping of is yeast.

Yeast?
Yes, yeast.

Yeast is an ingredient that is placed among the other elements to make the bread rise. Without yeast, you'd simply end up with flat, unleavened bread.

So how does yeast apply to life?
It's what activates us.

Yeast looks a lot like environmental issues, poverty, homelessness, child abuse and neglect, struggling students and schools, suicide, pollution, animal cruelty, hopelessness, etc. The yeast in our lives calls us to action, activating us for a cause. It is the very thing that takes us from concern for ourselves to concern for our community, for children of other nations, people trapped in modern day slavery, teens committing suicide and infant mortality. For the man or woman standing on the side of the road hungry to the child coming to school with holes in their clothing. It is the agent that takes everything that we've been through, that we've experienced, and makes us desire to do something with it.

We realize our flour has value.
Our sugar is needed
and that our salt gives us the kahunas to actually do something about it.

Like bread, if there weren't an activating agent in our lives, nothing would happen. If we never go beyond ourselves, then everything we've ever experienced or learned would be wasted. Like the flat, not so tasty bread, our lives would lack purpose and fulfillment. It is not until our hearts become open and aware of the needs of others that our lives take on an entirely new meaning.

And once we're activated, it's time to be kneaded.

As yeast it to activating us for a cause, the kneading process works out our kinks and character flaws. It's the refining process that we each must go through to be sure our attitude, character and intentions are in line. Have you ever met someone at the top of his or her game; the one that's young, cocky and/or arrogant? It doesn't matter how they got there. Whether it was the "who you know," epidemic or if they actually climbed the ranks extremely fast, their attitude still may suck. Unfortunately, they skipped the kneading process or forgot their process altogether.

Imagine for a second you're a large lump of dough. (Sorry, I know no one ever wants to imagine they are a large lump of anything, but stick with me.) As you step out on the journey to living your calling, you realize you still have to go to your job, deal with *those* people and complete *those* tasks. Unfortunately, just because you uncover what you were made to do, doesn't mean you get to jump right in and do it. The kneading process tends to be longer and trickier than any of its predecessors. If you are currently in a job that you don't love, you'll quickly realize that you may have to stay there in order to pay the bills. While it seems like the worse thing possible at the moment, when all you want to do is live out your dreams, stick in there. After all, someone has to feed Fido his favorite puppy snacks.

Let's get serious for a moment. You've discovered your dream and are ready to start living it out. You're excited, on fire and sharing with anyone who will listen your plans to change the world. Your nights are filled with restless sleep because your mind is making a list of all the things you must do, the places you must go and the people you'll have to recruit for the journey. It's great to be excited. I'm excited for you, but the truth is, it takes a little time to get from here to there.

The kneading process is not in place to make you annoyed. It's not there to make you want to give up and throw in the towel. The kneading process is a gift.

A gift?
Really?

Yes, I know. I saw it as anything but a gift as I embarked on my journey to, "who in the world am I supposed to be?" When I graduated from college with a degree in English, I truly thought I was hot stuff. It was rare to be an English major, intimidating even. We were the ones who thought writing papers were fun, engaging and a chance to explore some unknown territory. The art of rhetoric was a favorite past time; while writing and critiquing manuscripts happened to be a normal occurrence of life. As I journeyed through my senior year, I seemed to stumble upon my love of creative writing. It was like something else took over me as I wrote page after page, letting the main character drive the story; thickening the plot to a place I was even shocked to find us. It was a world like nothing I had ever experienced before and I loved it. But to make matters worse, so did my professors and classmates. They praised my ability to create dynamic characters, dialogue and realistic settings. And to my downfall, the praise made my head big.

Really, really big.

I set out to become the next best selling Young Adult author, spending days and nights writing a book that I was sure would be the next "Twilight" or "Harry Potter." I loved that book and those characters, but my attitude was in the wrong place. I felt entitled, superior and like my gift was solely for my own personal gain. And that's when it happened. My ability to write slowly drifted away. It didn't happen all at once. At first it started as not having the time, which shifted to loss of inspiration. As life became busier, the sight of my writing notebooks began to build stress, anxiety and angst. I knew I should be writing and creating, but teaching was so overwhelming that my capacity to do anything else was all but inexistent. And as I distanced myself from my love of the craft, I fell out of love. It became a looming beacon of failure. A once hoped for dream that would never ever amount to anything. Manuscripts sat stashed in my office desk, collecting dust and it was okay because clearly, I wasn't as good as I thought I was. And with that, I lost my love, I lost my gift and I lost the drive to create.

The feeling of utter failure loomed so great over me that even the thought of writing created anxiety. I didn't have writer's block; I just didn't want to write. Nothing inside of me could bring me to put words to paper. To be completely honest, this book has been a labor of finding my first love again. You see, even as I write to you, I'm in the kneading process. It's ongoing. When the topic of being more than our labels was put on my heart, I didn't know what it was supposed to be or look like, but I knew that I had to tell people about it. Had to use any way I could to help women find their personal purpose and calling. The difference between my writing to you today and if I would have wrote to you then is my heart. No longer is writing about what I can do for myself. What accolades or compliments I can get because the fact of the matter is, I'm just not that good. I'm not that good at anything that I do, but I try my hardest and always give my best. The kneading process pressed me, crushed me, smoothed me out and made sure no where in the mix did I think any of this was about me. It always has been and always will be about God and what He asks us to do. What we get to do.

So don't reject your kneading process. It truly is the preparation ground for all that has been prepared for you and it's the final step before you're placed in the theoretical oven.

Like any bread, the final step is to put it in a pan and bake it. The baking process is hot, takes time and is critical to having a great tasty outcome. Let's be real; unbaked bread dough is useless and not that tasty. The baking process of our lives includes the tests of our character and our opportunities to practice. It's the times when we're forced to step out of our comfort zone and really use our gifts to impact others. It happens in small ways at first. Maybe leading a training or small orientation of a few people. Maybe you're asked to write a review for your boss on a product or service. It could be that you get the opportunity to lead a special service project in the organization you've been volunteering with. Whatever your form of practice would look like, it's preparing you for when you emerge, fully prepared, fully equipped and fully confident that you now have what it takes to step out and take on the world.

The point of the final step in the process of our hypothetical award winning bread is that you are no longer searching for your meaning. At the point you come out of the oven, you absolutely know who you are, where you're going and what it will take to get there. And you know what the best part is? You'll have the right attitude to go along with the newly engrained force to change this world for the better and with that, you'll have a new appreciation for bread.

Chapter 6

❦

THE WHY BEHIND
YOUR WHAT

Whew, aren't you glad we made it through the process? We're almost there. Stick with me just a little longer. Isn't it exciting to finally know the "what" you've been called to do?

You may not know the *how*; that will unfold as you keep taking steps on your journey, but the *what* is what propels you into your destiny. I don't know what your specific what is, but I know that it will be glorious once you step into it. So what is this chapter about? What more can we possibly say about finding your calling?

Well, I'm glad you asked.

It no doubt wasn't an easy task to uncover your personal calling. To dig deep into your past, identity and challenges to find out just what you were placed here on this Earth to do. It took me years of struggles, failures and dashed dreams to get to here. Wherever here is. But when I take into account all that I've been blessed with, the privilege to speak, teach and write, I never want to forget the why behind the what.

What do I mean?

Every calling has a why behind it. A reason you got into doing it in the first place; the spark that ignited your dream or the strong desire to want to do more.

For me, the why behind my what came on a normal morning during my collegiate years as I sat on the couch in my living room. Flipping through the channels, my eyes caught a glimpse of a boat ramp at the Hudson River that had been taped off by yellow police caution tape. Plastered across the screen in red was, "Mother drives into river, kills 3 kids, 1 escapes." I sat there shocked and devastated as the news anchor unfolded the story. The night before, after an argument with a seemingly unfaithful boyfriend, LaShandra Armstrong, the mother of four beautiful young children, lost all hope.

Packing her children into their family mini-van, she drove into the Hudson River, killing herself and three of her four children. One child, the oldest, was able to roll down the window before the car was fully submerged by water and escape. He swam to shore where he was picked up by a woman who happened to be passing by. As she questioned his wetness and being out alone at that time of night, he explained to her the horrific event he had just endured.

My heart sank for that young child. For a ten year old who will forever have the image of his mother driving him and his family into the river on replay in his mind. The sounds of his siblings crying and screaming as the car crashed into the icy cold waters of the Hudson. And most awful of all, the aftermath of having to live a life without your mother because of one tragic incident, one moment of hopelessness, one bad decision made in an instance.

As I thought about LaShandra, as I still think about her, I can't help but feel responsible. Not that I would have ever met her, or even done anything to keep her from that fatal act, but for all the LaShandras out there. For all the women who feel all hope is lost. For the women who only know their value tied to a man, a career, a position, status, or physical appearance. For the young lady with tears in her eyes, a newborn at home and a husband who just admitted he's been having an affair over the last year and doesn't want her anymore. For the woman who jumps from relationship to relationship, trying to fill the voids of significance and love from an absent father in her life. Or finally, for the countless women prostituting themselves to quench a habit, appease a handler, or put food on the table. These women are my whys. I may never meet each and every one of them, but you could.

Someone you know can and will.

The *why* behind my *what* is to help women know who they are and whose they are so that they can go out and tell someone else. You see the words in this book are no mistake. They were thought about, prayed about and divinely put here on these pages so that every woman who picks it up would be ignited to go out and accomplish her what. But most importantly, these words are written to you right now as you sit quietly reading in your living room, at the coffee shop or the shoreline of the ocean, so that you will always remember the why behind your what. The why will be what keeps you moving forward. The deep burden of the why is what makes you fight harder, longer and more diligently.

If we were only ever given the what, we might do a little here or there and then move on to the next thing, but the why is what makes us never want to stop doing *this* thing. The thought of another woman losing hope and taking her life and the lives of her children is enough for me to say, "Okay, I did that. What can I do next?" It's not enough for me to write a few words on a page. I have to daily be on mission, looking for women who need a little pick me up or a word of encouragement.

Sometimes it's as simple as a text.

Others, it's a three hour unplanned meeting when my to-do list is forever growing. And still, there are the women's event, meetings or conferences where I am able to speak to hundreds of women, all with a different story, need, or hidden secret. It doesn't matter what my what looks like, the why behind me getting out of bed, walking slowly enough to notice a need, or talking with a random woman in Target for an hour is always the same.

There will be no more LaShandras on my watch.
On your watch.

Sure there will still be tragedy, don't get me wrong, but when there is an army of women mobilized and determined to change this world, the loss of life, identity and hope will be a lot less common.

One of my favorite speakers, who also happens to be a kick butt sex trafficking abolitionist, is an awesome woman from Australia. Her books, speaking engagements and daily podcasts continue to ignite women for their purpose, but there was an activating moment that changed everything for her. In many of her talks, she recounts the very conversation that revealed the why behind her what.

After rescuing a group of young girls out of a sex trafficking ring overseas, she along with some of her team went to meet with them. As they listened to each girls story, they were shocked at what they heard. The brutal circumstances which they endured were unfathomable. They listened intently and then it was her turn to share about grace, love and a promise for the future. She talked about the promises of God and the hope that can be found in Him. Her words were true, powerful and seemingly relevant, but to her surprise, one of the young ladies turned, looked her square in the face and stated, "If what you say about your God is true, why didn't you come sooner?"

Why didn't you come sooner; a phrase that not only echoes in her mind, but mine as well.

Why didn't we come sooner?
Why didn't I write sooner?
Why didn't we encourage sooner?
Give hope sooner?
Love and encourage more openly sooner?

What were we doing? What were we too busy with? Afraid of? So many times we know our what but simply do nothing about it; our excuses are limitless. We don't have the resources, we're unqualified, no one will help us, we have children and on and on. That simple yet piercing statement will never leave my heart and mind. Once we know our what and remember the why behind it, we need to go and step out.

The longer we wait, the more is lost.

So I want to give you a moment to reflect. Now that you know your what, what's the why behind it? It could be a family member, a friend, a student, a neighborhood child, a co-worker or someone you've never met. As you process, I want you to write down the why behind your what, but don't stop there. Think about what's holding you back and list that as well. I'll give you the time. Please don't skip over this activity. It will be the very thing that keeps propelling you forward.

What's the why behind your what?

_____

_____

_____

_____

_____

_____

_____

_____

_____

_____

What's holding you back?

_____

_____

_____

_____

_____

_____

_____

_____

_____

What can be the very thing that propels you forward?

_____

_____

_____

_____

_____

_____

_____

_____

_____

I hope this chapter was a much-needed stop for you as much as it has been for me. There is nothing more motivating to press on than to remember why you set off in the first place. Living in your calling is a wonderful place, but it can be as equally dangerous. When we keep our eye on the prize, our *whys* behind our *whats*, we can be assured that every decision we're making has the right heart and intention behind it. As you step out into your journey, never forget these pages. Never forget the reason you went in the first place.

And never ever fail to go sooner.

Chapter 7

LEAVE YOUR LUGGAGE BEHIND

There is nothing that makes me happier than the thrill of a new adventure outside of our county of residence. I love booking our family's flight to a new city where we will no doubt explore culture and indulge in the tastiest foods it has to offer, although we probably spend a lot more time eating than we do site seeing. While arriving at the destination is great, I don't exactly love the preparation it takes to get there. Packing suitcases for my wonderful husband, myself and a two year old isn't exactly the highlight of the trip. Not to mention the unpacking part. It's a little pathetic to admit, but mommy's luggage tends to sit in our room, staring at me so long that I'd rather burn it than put it away.

You see, it's easy to put the stuff in, exciting even. There's the essentials, underwear (can't forget those), jeans, tops, coats, shoes, shoes, hats, oh and did I bring enough shoes? And like any woman knows, no outfit is complete without accessories, so in goes the earrings, necklaces, watches, and scarves; so many colorfully fun scarves. Oh what a joy it is to step back and see the array of colors. The fun to be had in this new exciting city, the freeness it is to dress however because no one knows you. Yes. We need to take that piece too!

The problem isn't in the packing. It's what happens when the suitcase is zipped up, stood upright and then gawked at by my suspecting husband. The reaction is always the same. "Babe, I'm pretty sure your suitcase is overweight," to which I say absolutely not. There's no way. I only brought the essentials.

Isn't that just how life is? As we move on to a new place and space in our calling, we pull out our huge rolling luggage and pack everything in; taking this and that. They're all just essentials after all, right?

That friend we know isn't the best fit for our future.
That guy who pulls us down instead of lifting us up.
That salary that is a nice cushion but it eats away at all our extra time.
That position that gives us a sense of purpose and meaning.
Those brands because they mean we've made it.

What's your form of security? What are you throwing into your suitcase and trying to drag along with you as you step into the next part of your life?

You know what's funny about suitcases? There are so many nooks and crannies that things can go into. We can stuff, stuff and stuff some more until every single square inch is occupied. The problem is, the more we fill that piece of luggage, the heavier it gets. And like checking onto a flight, eventually that luggage will have to be weighed. The heavier it is, the more it will cost you. While it's natural to bring some things from one stage of life into the next, we have to be very careful just what comes with us.

To be honest, our transition into our new calling should look a lot more like an overnight trip than a weeklong excursion. (It's a good thing there are a lot of fabulous weekender bags out there. Just saying.)

When we step into our calling, things tend to move a lot faster. Two well-respected women I know and love like to refer to it as the "crazy train." When life calls for decisions, stepping out in faith and moving forward, we cannot have a sixty-pound bag holding us back. Keeping us from being able to say yes because we're responsible for this or that. When we finally step into our calling, it is vital that we leave our luggage behind. It's the only way we'll ever reach our full potential. I love these lyrics by Dara Maclean from her song *Suitcases:*

How can you move when they're weighing you down?
What can you do when you're tied to the ground?

Yeahyou carry your burdens,

Heavy like gravity
Just let them go now,

There's freedom in release

You can't run when you're holding suitcases
It's a new day throw away your mistakes

and open up your heart,
lay down your guard,
you don't have to be afraid.

Isn't that what it really comes down to?

We stick as much as we can in our suitcases at the fear of

being unprepared and ill-equipped. If we take everything with us, we'll have a much better chance at being successful, right? Not really. Would it be of benefit to take the negative voices and relationships with us? The financial status when it gives us a prideful, haughty attitude? The questioning peanut gallery who just don't understand why we would give up all of this to go and do *that*? But most importantly, we must leave our suitcases behind because it shows that we are finally stepping out in true faith. We're leaving all our options behind and saying, "God, this was your idea. Do what only you can do." It's then and only then that we experience the fullness of what He can do.

The other day while driving down the highway, I heard a great reminder of just how dangerous it is to carry things along with us even when we know we should leave it behind. A great man named Paul set out to sea along with a convoy of other men. As they ventured to their destination, a strong wind they were hoping would carry them along to their desired point turned dangerous, making them lose control of the ship. Prior to taking on this wind, Paul warned the crew that it wouldn't be a good idea to try to sail in such bad weather, but they pressed forward anyway. As the ship ran its course, each man feared the worse. Without full control of the ship, they would certainly die. As Paul watched the despair on their faces, he prayed and believed that they would be spared. Finally, taking a stand and speaking with authority, Paul instructed them on how they were to conduct themselves in order to stop the loss, which at that point seemed inevitable.

A vital part of every ship was something called a skiff. The skiff would float behind the boat and be a sense of security for the crew if anything were to happen to the main vessel. This skiff was the guarantee that some would live while others would perish, not very reassuring if you ask me. As the weather turned from bad to worse, a few men began boarding the skiff, determined to leave the doomed ship and take their chances out on the rough waters. As they prepared to lower themselves down, Paul warned them that if they used that skiff, if they chose the seeming security over faith, that they would be saved, everyone aboard the ship would die; those on the skiff included. Hearing the authority and finality in Paul's voice, the men climbed out of the small vessel, trusting that the words he spoke were true. That while the skiff seemed like a lifesaver, it would inevitably lead to their demise.

Are you like the sailors on that boat? Ready to jump ship as soon as the waters get rough?

If so, what is your skiff? What's that little thing that drags behind you, securing your future from the unforeseen destruction that could be ahead?

_____

_____

_____

Isn't that what it comes down to? The what ifs and how's?
What if I quit my job? What will I do?
What if this idea doesn't actually work?
What if I stop sleeping with him and he actually leaves?
What if I'm a terrible mom?
What if my students hate me?
What if I disappoint him or her?
What if I'm just not good enough?

The skiff we allow to drag behind us is nothing more than a suitcase. It's a life raft just in case *those* plans don't actually work out. I have one. I'm sure you do too, but it's time to cut it away.

It's time for us to get rid of our safety nets and back up plans, watching them float away, and determine that forward is the only way to go. Nothing behind us is going to be better than the life that is before us as we step into our calling.

⁂

Recently I had the strong urge to clean and declutter my home office. An office that up until a few weeks ago had been unusable because it was buried under mounds of birthday decor, family junk, toddler ride on cars, home décor and whatever else had been thrown in there. A place that was meant to be mommy's retreat became mommy's worst nightmare. Needless to say, the last thing I wanted to do on a Saturday afternoon was clean such a disastrous place, but clean I did. No matter how much I convinced myself of the many other things there was to do around the house, for some reason I felt this draw to go traverse the jungle.

As I began digging around, throwing out this, storing that and relocating things to the outside shed that I'm sure my husband snuck in, inspiration and life began to fill my heart. Promises scribbled on sticky notes that I had completely forgotten about were renewed, and best of all, I could see my desk. But just like everything in life, the real reason I was drawn into my office began to surface.

As I dug around in the closet, I mistakenly tugged on the light string that was hanging quite low. I was startled as the light bulb beamed, illuminating the entire closet. Yes, I've avoided this very office so long that I forgot the closet even had a light in it. Peering at the jam-packed shelves hanging overhead, a looming stack of books and binders immediately caught my eye. I was shocked. Sitting there overhead was curriculum upon curriculum from my days as an English teacher. To paint the enormity of the situation for you, they were taking up at least half of the upper closet storage space.

To make matters worse, as I shifted my attention to the clutter and mayhem below, I noticed the six stacked paper ream boxes that were storing what was my former reading library along with various classroom supplies. Unbeknownst to me, I had been secretly carrying my former security into my future; the all to familiar back up plan, just in case this whole calling thing didn't work out. To put it lightly, I was mortified. What I thought was a scary adventure into an overflowing office was really a revelation of all the stuff I was carrying around in my suitcase.

The reality is that sometimes we can be carrying around things in our suitcases that we have no idea are even there. Things we may have buried deep in the corners of our minds, slowly creep their way to the surface when uncertainty begins to set in.

And uncertainty always sets in.

In my horror, I did what I do best, picked up my cell phone and called my best friend. As my sister answered her phone, our conversation went a little like this:

"Hey, are you going to become a teacher or go back to being a police officer?"

"Um, probably a teacher. Why?"

"What subject? Middle or high school?"

"History or social studies, why?"

"Perfect! I have to get rid of all this stuff."

It was ten o'clock at night. She probably thought I was crazy, but that's okay because I had to get rid of that stuff. As

I explained my reason for calling, she gasped in horror as she too realized if she was going to step into her calling, she would have to give up her police belt and chic pink handcuffs; her ultimate sense of authority and power.

I have to admit that her items are a lot more weighty than my curriculum books, but in order to move into our future, we have to shed all the unnecessary weight.

It is impossible to move into our future when we're still holding on so tightly to our past.

I think this is a perfect time for me to be quiet and give you a chance to reflect. As you ponder the idea of your personal suitcase, what are some things that you're carrying around with you, trying to take into your future just in case *that* plan doesn't work out?

_____

_____

_____

_____

Take a moment and dig a little deeper. It may take some scrolling through contacts in your phone, rummaging around in storage, or sifting through your social media, but what may be something or someone that you have been inadvertently carrying into your future?

_____

_____

_____

_____

What are some steps you can take to resolve that situation today, right at this moment? There really isn't a better time to make a decision for your future than right now when you're living, breathing and contemplating your next steps.

Write your next three action steps below.

1. _____
   _____
   _____

2. _____
   _____
   _____

3. _____
   _____
   _____

As you apply those first three steps this week, you will no doubt feel some sort of pain or feeling of resistance as you cut away your skiff, empty out your suitcase and prepare to embark on the journey that has been so beautifully marked out for you. There is no time like now to make those changes. By releasing the things that keep us secure, that keeps our resolve teetering between all in and the safe zone, we can confidently step out in faith without ever looking back to what could have been. My friend, your future will always be a lot better than the past you left behind. It might take some fighting, some motivating and a whole lot of work, but you will get there.

And in the end, when you're living a life of fulfillment that you could have never dreamt of, you'll be so ecstatic that you made the decision right here in this very moment, to leave your luggage behind.

Chapter 8

※

MORE THAN: YOU ARE A LION, NOT A POODLE

I can't think of a more fitting way to conclude our time together than to end where we started. To remind you, to remind me, that we are so much more than our current circumstance, a past label, a failed dream, or a negative word or words that have been spoken over us. Once we allow those labels to be removed, ourselves to be relabeled for a cause and to start to identify ourselves the way that God identifies us, then and only then can we begin to discover our calling.

As important as all these chapters have been in how to get from here to there, the most important thing is to know who we are. It is only when we know who we are that we will ever be able to go out and let those who are lost and broken know who they are. We can't rescue in our brokenness. We cannot rescue when we lack identity. We can only rescue others when we ourselves have been made whole. When we have discovered that we are so much more than our labels.

You are so much more than your labels.

I love this quote from author and speaker, Steven Furtick:

"Until you know who you are,
you will never know what to do."

So where do we go from here?

How do we take our newfound identities and walk in the fullness and greatness of the callings on our lives?

If there's one thing I know, it's that it will not be easy. Not everyone will be okay with letting go of who you were to embrace this new you, this confident you, but will you make me a promise? Will you remember what you read here on these pages? Will you not file this book amongst the dusting, decaying books on your shelves? I pray that this book will be a resource for you at every new stage of your life. That it will be a reference point once you get into one of those seasons when you feel lost, frustrated, or confused. That you will remember the things you wrote on these pages. The quiet moments of heart discovery and that those very moments will reignite the fire and passion of the seed that has been placed in your heart.

Will you promise me that?
Let's make a pact right here together.
Let's sign our names and confirm that yes, we will live in this new calling, that we will live boldly and fearlessly.

Are you ready? Good.

I'll go first.

Vonae Deyshawn

Beautiful You

There's no going back from here.

I want to hold you accountable and I hope that you will do the same for me. We will call it our Forward Pact, because whatever is in front of you when you're walking in your calling will always be better than what has been behind you.

As I think back on this book and how far we've come, I'm so grateful that you stuck with it. The journey of self-discovery is never an easy one, but it is a fulfilling one. I hope this book has been just as revealing and transforming for you as it has been for me. That it challenges you to step up and step out. That when you remember who you were called to be, you would walk confidently and boldly in that revelation.

So how will we do just that?

We will remember that we are lions and not poodles?

Wait?
That's the secret?
Well sort of. Let me explain.

When I reflect on who I was last year compared with who

I am today, the difference is staggering. Through many prayers for boldness, believing I was more than any label people could put on me and walking confidently, my personality has shifted and molded drastically. As I walked in this new boldness, I realized rather quickly that the ease in which I previously fit into my surroundings began to change. This new confidence unbeknownst to me became evident to those around me. Some accepted it, while others tried unsuccessfully to stick me back in the place I once was. It was one evening where I sat on my couch watching an online speaker that the concept of being a lion and not a poodle hit me in the face.

The story was of a lion cub rescued after poachers killed his mother, taken home and then house broken. The cub spent his early years under the care and influence of the house poodle. He learned to prance around, use the bathroom outside, eat his meals out of a fancy doggie bowl and cower at the neighbor's large Rottweiler. Those years were spent restrained by a simple chain linked fence, a structure that proved to be daunting for a simple poodle, but an absolute joke for a lion. Well, for a lion that happened to know who and what he was made for.

As years passed, the cub grew bigger and stronger. He began to notice that his stature was different. Instead of the small dainty paws that the poodle possessed, he boasted large paws with claws that would tear the furniture and rugs, sending him outside on punishment. Then all of a sudden, a thick mass of fur surrounded his face, confusing his sense of identity. What was happening to him? Why was he beginning to look so different from his brother? From the only family he had ever known?

While he was changing physically, something also began happening in his heart. He began to become uneasy, disconnected and unsatisfied from his current situation. He found himself looking beyond the fence to a jungle he had never noticed before. The lush green scenery just beyond his current boundary began to beckon to him. He longed for freedom, for the chance to run, for the chance to hunt. His innate instincts were beginning to manifest, digging up all the things he was always meant to be and do.

As he sat one night, looking off into the distance, wanting to burst out of his confinement, he heard it. He heard the very noise that would change his life forever. In the far off distance, in the very same lush greenery of the jungle he had longed for, came a deep, commanding roar of a lion. A lion that was strong, confident and free. Hearing the roar again, our lion friend stood to his feet, his heart racing and a new hope filling his body. All of a sudden, a new confidence came upon him and he returned the roar. That was it. That was the secret. For so long he had been confined by his surroundings, not knowing that he had been built for speed, stamina and strength. With a long, deep stride, he bounded over the very fence that kept him confined for so many years.

Finally, he was free to live the life he was always meant to. Free to run, free to hunt and free to boldly declare that he is the king of the jungle!

I think from time to time, we all get a slight case of poodle syndrome. Sometimes it happens unexpectedly, while other times we purposely try to mold and fit ourselves into a situation, social scene or opportunity that we were never meant for; whether that is to try and prove ourselves or if we just simply fall into an opportunity that we find hard to get out of. Whatever the situation, you must always remember you are a lion, not a poodle.

As I began on reflecting on who I was in this season, I kept hearing a simple phrase repeated over and over, "Do you even know who you are?"

Do you even know who you are?

It's so vital as we step into our next seasons that we know who we are. That we are the person we were told to be and not who everyone else wants us to be. If there is one thing that I have discovered, it's that not every situation is bad for you. Not every path is going to lead you to a terrible, destructive future. No, there are absolute good paths and good opportunities that will present themselves to you. The difference in being a lion and a poodle is that you are able to distinguish between the two paths. Like the lion, he could have stayed in the comfort of his current situation. He was well fed, safe and had all the comforts and amenities he could ever want, but that was only a good path. As he broke free and lived in the fullness of who he was created to be, he began walking on the great path that had always been meant for him. In life, there will always be a good path, but God wants you to take the great path.

The great path leads to fulfillment, abundance and life. The good path is safe, substantial, but fulfillment only lasts for a period of time. Eventually, like the lion, you will become restless, unfulfilled and begin to wonder if there could be more to life than this. I don't know about you, but I'd rather live like a lion any day than like a confined poodle.

So as we end our time together, will you bound into the future as a strong, confident lion, fully embracing the call and plan for your life? Will you leave behind your luggage and the security of knowing the next step in order to trust that His plan is greater than anything we could ever come up with? If so, you can rest assure that you have a father in Heaven who loves you, will never abandon you and will walk alongside you as you take those steps to live out His calling for your life.

Be blessed, walk in your calling and always remember that you are more than any label you or anyone else could ever put on you.

VONAE DEYSHAWN

That the truest thing about you is what God says about you.

ADEQUACY:
A SPECIAL NOTE FROM VONAE

When was the last time you doubted your ability to do something? Land a job, make a good impression, give a presentation, make someone proud, or simply cook a good meal?

I say simply, but who am I kidding?

I'm probably the only woman in America who has to pray while prepping a meal, cooking it, and as I put it down on the table; pleading with God to please let it taste good so that my toddler doesn't send it crashing to the floor. I'll admit it, I suffer from a severe case of cooking deficiency or dare I say it . . . inadequacy.

If we're being honest, don't we all suffer from feelings of being anything but adequate from time to time? What does it mean to be adequate anyway? Why on Earth does it matter? And most importantly, you're probably wondering why I'm making such a huge fuss about it?

My hope is that you would find hope, meaning and value in this life, and frankly there's no better place to start than the subject of adequacy.

Adequate . . . A simple eight letter word meaning,

Enough for some need or requirement.
Or put another way,
 The state of being good enough!

Thank you Webster.

And there it is. A word whose meaning is the exact opposite of the way we view ourselves in different situations, seasons and positions in life. Of course we know its meaning as we use it casually in everyday conversation, but why does the reality seem so illusive and impossible for us to hang on to?

You see, although we find each minute flaw of ours, we have a heavenly father who says we are enough.

You my friend are enough!

Instead of measuring our worth on our position, career title, the house we live in, or the car we drive, God wants us to see ourselves the way He does. I love the constant whisper in my heart, "You are more than enough."

Unfortunately, it is all too easy to fall into feelings of inadequacy. We look at our lives and compare it to *her*. You know, that gorgeous girl everyone wants to be friends with. The top executive who always has a clever answer that makes everyone laugh. The writer who gets to travel for a living, getting paid to jet set while chronicling her adventures in fashion. Those girls, they have it all together. They're qualified, dignified and all around fabulous.

Who could ever compare to them?
Me?
No, never.

I know this feeling all too well. Yes, I struggle with inadequacy too and so does that "perfect" girl. And you probably thought I had it all figured out. Not quite.

In the past few months, I had the opportunity to transition into a new position within the organization I work for. At first I was ecstatic! Ideas, dreams and goals poured in from all sides.

I could do this job with my eyes closed.

Or so I thought. The internal and external voices reminding me just how unqualified I was certainly didn't help. Although the position was something I had been doing in a smaller capacity within the organization for six years, once it became my career, I could think of a thousand reasons I shouldn't in fact be doing it. I mean seriously, who would trust me to give others advice?

As I struggled with the looming weight of inadequacy, I felt God say, "Would you just stop! You don't have to be anyone different than who I've created you to be. You were chosen because of who you are, your passion and what you're already doing. Just be you."

That was the key that released me from my plague of not being good enough.

I was chosen because of my personality, passion and drive. While some gawked at my placement in the new role, I began to understand that it wasn't because of how much theology I could rattle off, but because I cared. I may never be able to spout information from the top of my head like the next expert, but I can love people and make them feel cared about. In short, I can be good at being me.

Not someone else.

Inadequacy, a word meaning lacking the quality or quantity required; insufficient for a purpose, is the exact opposite. It's the state of not being enough for a purpose. It's overwhelming, daunting and crippling. Inadequacy keeps us in the place we are in right at this moment. Frozen in time, afraid to take a step forward or back; just there.

It's like a heavy weight pressing down on us from all sides. Do you feel it? Those voices telling you that you couldn't possibly get that job promotion or lead that team of men? That the investment you were seeking wont ever be yours because *that* company historically doesn't fund women. Or maybe you're a working mom, feeling the guilt of having to leave your child while your friends stay home doing the "professional mommy" thing. They don't mean to, but the guilt trip they provide because you have to work for a living cripples your heart.

There are entirely too many opportunities to feel less than. Too many opportunities to point to our weaknesses and say, "See, see! This is why I can't accomplish this or that. I am a woman. I am a mom. I am a teacher. I'm not paid enough. I'm the only woman in my organization. They don't respect women . . ."

And the list goes on.

In order to reach a place of knowing that we are more than enough, we have to accept it for ourselves. No one will ever make us know the truth that God created us for a purpose and specific calling; that we are   beautifully and wonderfully made and because of that reality, we can overcome anything that is thrown at us. We must accept the truth that we are more than enough despite what a teacher, parent, spouse, co-worker or ex-boyfriend has spoken over our lives. When we embrace that truth we will be free to live in the promise that we are and always will be

Adequate.

Vonae Deyshawn

ABOUT THE AUTHOR

Vonae Deyshawn is a wife, mother and author who lives to inspire and empower others. A former educator, she spends her time writing, raising her son, being a wife to her wonderful husband and providing practical steps for a better life through life coaching. When she is not curled up in a bookstore sipping a Frappucino, she enjoys traveling and speaking at universities, conferences and retreats.

Virtue Media, an indie publishing company, is a long time dream realized and reflects Vonae's heart and motivation for life. Her desire is that every woman would find hope, purpose and the ability to live out their calling.

www.ingramcontent.com/pod-product-compliance
Lightning Source LLC
Chambersburg PA
CBHW061153040426
42445CB00013B/1670